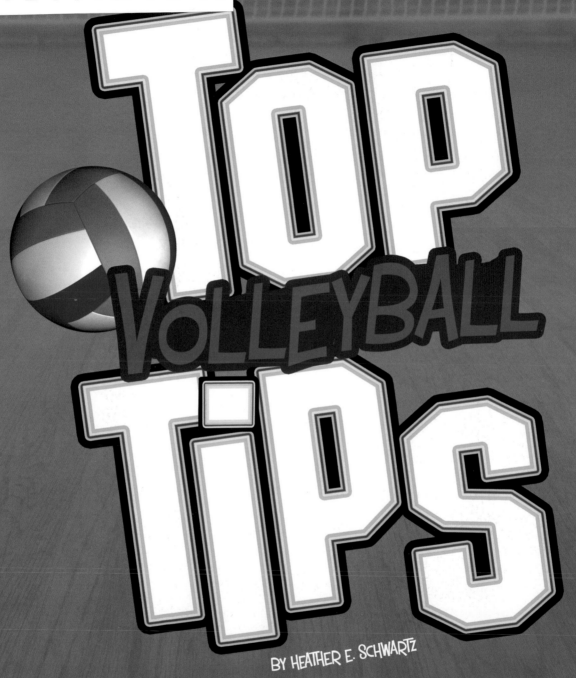

TOP VOLLEYBALL TIPS

BY HEATHER E. SCHWARTZ

Consultant: William Tatge
Head Women's Volleyball Coach, Lees-McRae College
Banner Elk, North Carolina

CAPSTONE PRESS
a capstone imprint

Snap Books are published by Capstone Press
1710 Roe Crest Drive, North Mankato, Minnesota 56003
www.mycapstone.com

Library of Congress Cataloging-in-Publication Data
Names: Schwartz, Heather E., author.
Title: Top volleyball tips / by Heather E. Schwartz.
Description: North Mankato, Minnesota : An imprint of Capstone Press, [2017]
   | Series: Snap Books. Top Sports Tips | Includes bibliographical
   references and index. | Audience: Ages: 8–14. | Audience: Grades: 4 to 6.
Identifiers: LCCN 2016026026| ISBN 9781515747208 (Library Binding) | ISBN
   9781515747260 (Paperback) | ISBN 9781515747444 (eBook PDF)
Subjects: LCSH: Volleyball—Juvenile literature.
Classification: LCC GV1015.34 .S39 2017 | DDC 796.325—dc23
LC record available at https://lccn.loc.gov/2016026026

EDITORIAL CREDITS

Editor: Gena Chester
Designer: Veronica Scott
Media Researcher: Eric Gohl
Production Specialist: Kathy McColley

PHOTO CREDITS

Capstone Studio: Karon Dubke, 9 (left), 11, 15, 23, 24, 25, 29 (top); Getty Images: The Washington Post, 8 (bottom); Newscom: Cal Sport Media/Michael Spomer, 17 (right), Icon SMI/Carrie Jesenovec, 26, ZUMA Press/Adolphe Pierre-Louis, 29 (bottom), ZUMA Press/Carolyn Van Houten, 21; Shutterstock: Aspen Photo, 16, 19, Mitrofanov Alexander, 4–5, 22, muzsy, 13, Pukhov Konstantin, 20, Ronnie Chua (volleyball court background), Ufuk Zivana, cover (volleyball), 1, 6, 8 (top), 9 (right), 10, 14, 17 (left), 18, 27, 32

Printed and bound in Canada
10040S17FR

TABLE OF CONTENTS

Ready, Set, Score!

Your body is tense as you watch the opposing team and wait for the serve. Smack! The ball sails over the net to the player next to you. She sets it up, and then it's your turn. Your fingertips push the ball up into the air. It comes down in perfect position for the middle hitter in the front row. She jumps up and attacks the ball with the palm of her hand. The ball hits the floor before your opponents can return it. Your team scores!

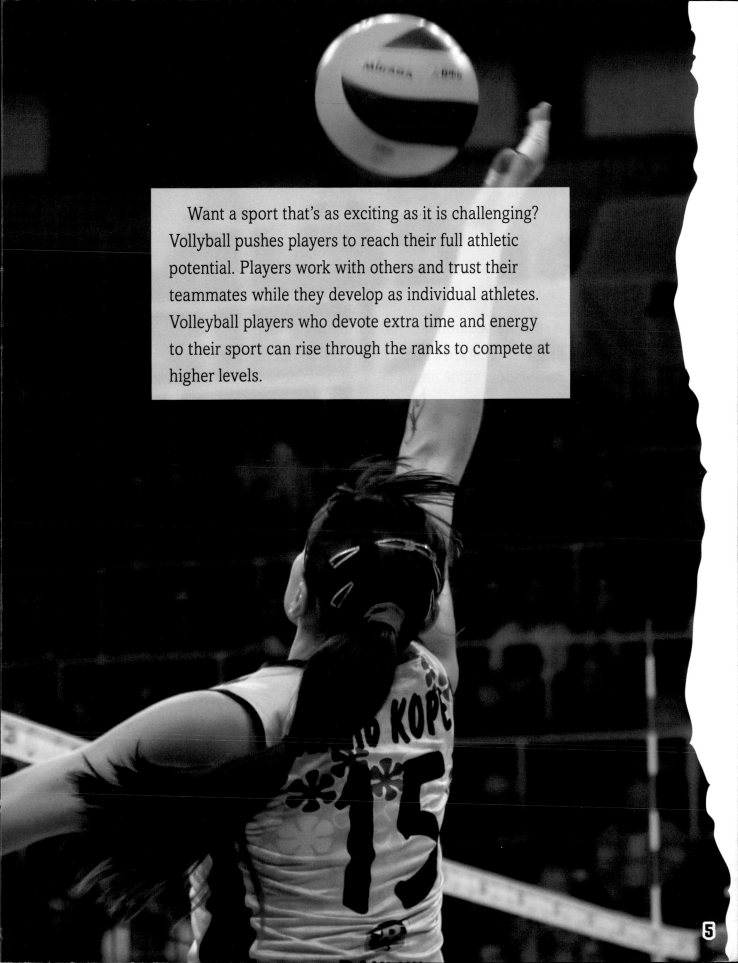

Want a sport that's as exciting as it is challenging? Vollyball pushes players to reach their full athletic potential. Players work with others and trust their teammates while they develop as individual athletes. Volleyball players who devote extra time and energy to their sport can rise through the ranks to compete at higher levels.

Score!

Volleyball players are super focused and always on their game. They can't look away or let their mind wander. When the ball is in motion, they have less than a second to react and win—or lose—the point.

One team serves the ball over the net to put it into play for a **rally**. The other team can touch the ball up to three times to return it over the net. Teammates pass the ball to set up the return. They often jump and **attack** the ball on their third touch. This makes it difficult for their opponents to send it back.

Each team scores a point whenever the opposing team doesn't return the ball inbounds correctly. The winning team wins the most **sets** out of five. The first four are scored up to 25 points. The fifth set is scored up to 15 points. Play continues, however, until one team wins by two points.

HISTORY OF THE *Sport*

Volleyball started out as a sport in 1895. William G. Morgan invented it. Morgan was a physical education director at the YMCA in Holyoke, Massachusetts. He called his new game Mintonette.

The game was originally meant for leisure. But it became more competitive over time. In 1949 the first World Championships in volleyball were held in Czechoslovakia.

Volleyball became an Olympic sport in 1964. Beach volleyball became an Olympic sport in 1996.

rally—the time between a serve and the end of play

attack—a forceful hit to return the ball over the net

set—a game played to a predetermined number of points; another meaning is to push the ball using only your fingertips

Chapter 2

POWER *Moves*

When a player serves the ball, she stands at the back of the court and behind the end line. Whether serving underhand or overhand, she has to hit the ball hard enough to send it over the net to land inbounds. Serving requires power and accuracy.

Work Your Serve

If you are right-handed, start by learning to serve underhand. Hold the ball in your left hand. Step forward with your left foot. If you are left-handed, start with the ball in your right hand and step with your right foot. While stepping forward, swing your other arm toward the ball. The faster you swing your arm, the more power the serve has. Keep your arm straight and hit the ball with the end of your palm and start of your wrist. The direction the ball goes depends on where you hit the ball.

When you're comfortable, work on your overhand serve. If you're right-handed, stand with your left foot forward and your right foot back. Hold the ball in front of you in your left hand. Toss it straight up about 2 feet (0.6 meters) into the air. At the same time, pull your right arm back by your ear. Bring it forward to hit the ball with your palm. Switch if you're left-handed. Practice hitting the ball at the right height. If you hit the ball too low, it won't go over the net. But if you hit the ball too high, it could sail out of bounds.

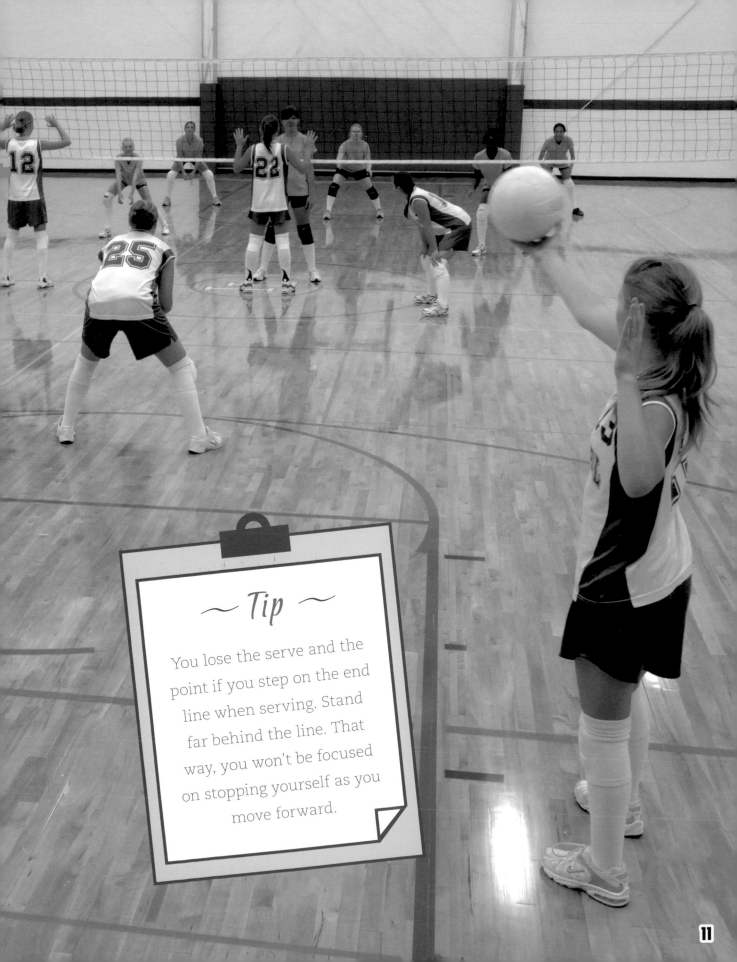

11

~ *Tip* ~

You lose the serve and the point if you step on the end line when serving. Stand far behind the line. That way, you won't be focused on stopping yourself as you move forward.

Chapter 3

TRUST
in Teamwork

Volleyball players may have excellent individual skills. But they also need to work as part of a team. Effective teamwork requires good communication skills. Without them, teammates risk colliding if two or more players go for the ball at the same time. They also risk giving a point to the other team. The ball will hit the ground if everyone assumes someone else is going to get it. Volleyball players do communication drills to make sure they understand one another during games.

Communication on the Court

Counting how many times your team contacts the ball can help you and your teammates talk during games. Stand on both sides of the court in two teams of three. Try to pass the ball and have it contact each player before sending it over the net. Count out loud each time your team contacts with the ball. Each contact is a point if you can successfully return the ball. The first team to reach 25 points wins.

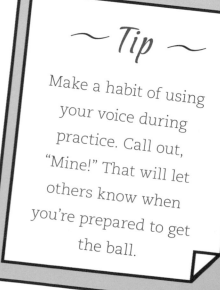

~ Tip ~

Make a habit of using your voice during practice. Call out, "Mine!" That will let others know when you're prepared to get the ball.

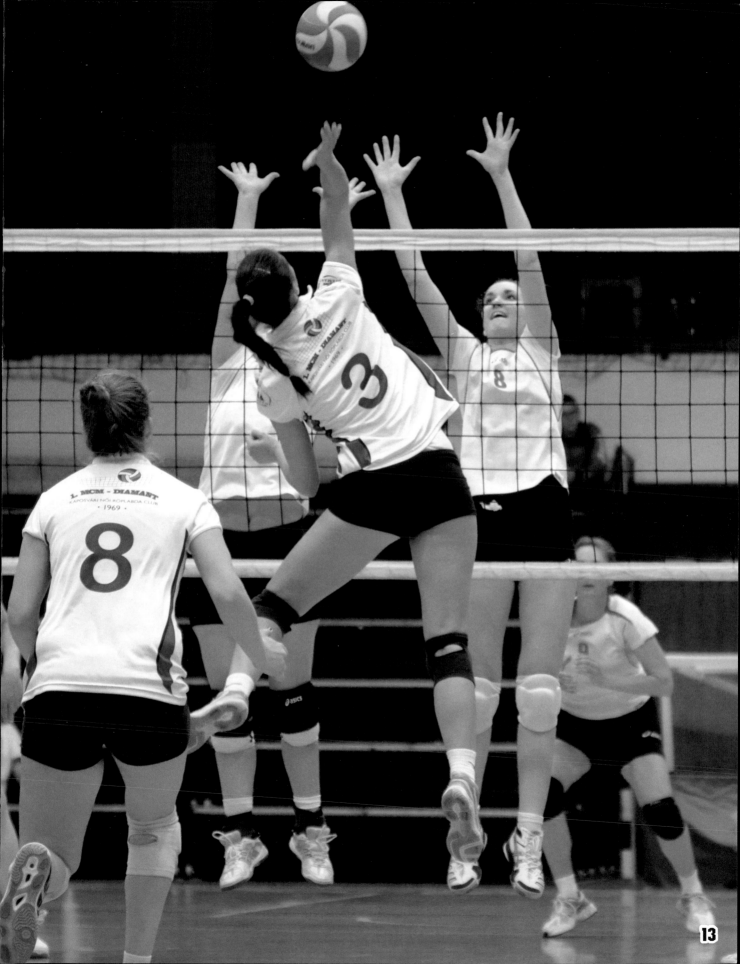

Pass the Ball

The first contact of the ball after the serve is the pass. A player contacts the ball with her forearms to pass it to a setter. The pass must be accurate, so the setter and hitter can do their jobs.

Prepare to Pass

Pass in place to develop a sense of where the ball should hit your forearms. Try to hit it high up in the air. Pass the ball as many times you can in a row on your own or with a partner.

Grab a partner and trash can, and head to the volleyball court! Place the trash can on your side toward the front of your net. Have your partner serve the volleyball to you from the other end of the court. Pass the ball with your forearms. Aim for the trash can. It's a good pass if it goes in or hits the rim. Switch so your partner gets the same chance to practice accuracy.

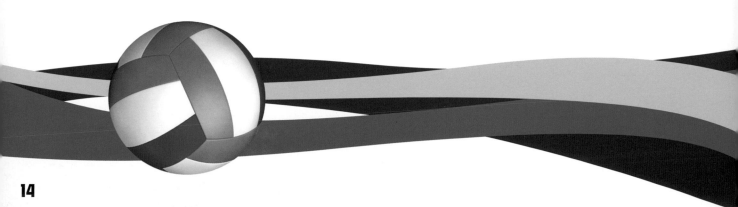

Set it Up

The setter contacts the ball second. Her fingers are spread out, with her pointer fingers and thumbs creating a triangle above her forehead. Setters prefer accurate passes so they can send easy sets to hitters. But what if the pass is too low? What if it comes in behind her? Working as a team means making the best of even those bad situations. Setters can learn to handle any kind of pass with practice.

~ Tip ~

You'll be a better setter if you talk to your teammates. Ask your team's hitters where they like their sets to be for optimal attacks.

Drills for Skills

Develop your footwork by practicing without a ball. This will prepare you to move to the ball if the pass comes in low or behind you. Run forward three steps, starting with your left foot. Pivot on your left toe and plant your left foot. At the same time, put your arms up and reach as if hitting the ball.

Strengthen your hands and wrists so you have better control of the ball. Stand 20 feet (6 m) from a partner on the same side of the net. Set the ball back and forth to each other, using your fingertips, arms, and legs for power.

How to Attack

The best volleyball players have great hitting skills. They combine aim, arm swing, and power to drill a ball over the net. With practice players can develop their technique to put even more force behind the ball.

Aim for Accuracy

Work on your aim and practice your arm swing at the same time by marking a spot on the wall. Stand about 10 feet (3 m) away. Toss the ball up in the air. Bring your arms up to hit the ball. Aim the ball at the spot on the wall.

Power Play

You can gain power in your attack with practice too. Stand about 10 feet (3 m) away from the wall. Hit the ball with an open palm toward the base where the wall meets the floor. Hit the ball hard enough so it bounces up when it hits the floor. Continue the drill by attacking the ball again as it bounces back to you from the wall.

~ *Tip* ~

Keep your eyes open! Watch your hand make contact with the ball. This helps you have solid contact. It also gives you a good view of where your opponent is trying to block.

MECHANICS *Matter*

Just like in serving, attacking takes power and accuracy. Volleyball players put **momentum** to work every step of the way. It all happens in an instant.

Volleyball players take an approach by stepping forward before they jump. For a right-handed hitter, the first step is with the right foot. Then the player takes three more steps and jumps. A left-handed player would start an approach with the left foot.

As players jump up, they swing their arms forward and up. This motion creates momentum for an increased **vertical** jump. While they're in the air, they swing their arms back behind their head and down to build power for a hard hit. When they finally hit the ball, all of the energy they've created goes into the attack.

momentum—the strength or force something has while it is moving

vertical—straight up and down

Chapter 4

ROCK THOSE
Reflexes

Volleyball is a fast-paced game. The ball travels all over the court within seconds. Players have to be able to keep up. They need quick reflexes and strong bodies to block, pass, set, and attack.

Faster Footwork

Warm up your footwork with shuffles. Set up cones about 30 feet (9 m) apart, or use the sidelines on a volleyball court. Start at one end. Shuffle your feet until you reach the other cone or line. Then, shuffle your feet in the opposite direction to return. Repeat back and forth.

Add a partner to continue working your reflexes. Stand on opposite sides of the net. Follow hand signals from your partner to sprint forward, back, left, and right. She should change the signals every three to five seconds. Switch roles to give your partner some practice.

Quick Recovery

Swift movements require more than fast reflexes in volleyball. Players also need to be able to switch with speed from one movement to the next. They have to recover quickly after they block, attack, or dive.

Learn to Recover

Work with teammates for practice. Have a passer, setter, and hitter on one side of the net and two blockers on the other. An extra player stands off to the side. The passer starts by sending the ball to the setter, who sets it up to the hitter. After she attacks, two players on the other side try to block the hit. If the block is successful, the hitter, setter, and passer will have to recover the ball before it hits the ground. If the block isn't successful, the extra player will toss in a second ball which they will have to recover instead.

Always Agile

Volleyball players need to be **agile** to put their reflexes and recovery skills into action during a game. Reaction-time drills help them build agility as well as quicker reflexes.

Training for agility does more than help players move quickly on the court. It also helps prevent injury. Agility drills teach players to make controlled movements when they are changing direction, jumping, and landing.

Cone Jumps

Line up five cones about 1 foot (0.3 m) apart. Stand on one side of the first cone. Jump sideways over the cone. Do the same over the second cone. Continue to the end of the line. Keep your hips forward and shoulders over your hips while you jump. Place both feet down at the same time.

Shuttle Runs

Shuttle runs train your feet to move quickly in different directions. Set up three cones about 15 feet (5 m) apart. Sprint from the first one to the second one. Sprint back. Then sprint from the first one to the third one. Sprint back. Rest and repeat.

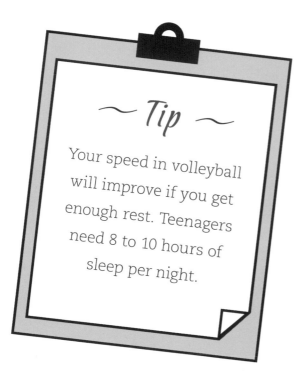

~ Tip ~

Your speed in volleyball will improve if you get enough rest. Teenagers need 8 to 10 hours of sleep per night.

agile—able to move quickly and easily
dynamic—involves motion
static—does not involve motion

INJURY *Prevention*

Athletes can also prevent injury by increasing their flexibility. Flexibility training, which includes **dynamic** and **static** stretches, increases range of motion in joints and muscles. Flexible volleyball players can bend and stretch easily to react quickly during games.

Chapter 5

OUTLAST YOUR *Opponents*

Stamina helps volleyball players stay in a fast-paced game to the end—with winning results. Players with good stamina can perform quick movements over and over without tiring out. Players gain stamina through training.

Wall Blocks

Blocking attacks throughout a volleyball game requires muscle strength and stamina. Mark an outside wall to the height of the volleyball net. Face the wall. Jump up and raise your arms as if blocking at the top of the net. Continue for three to five minutes at a quick pace. Try it from a squatting position at a slower pace.

Skater Jumps

Start with your hands out to your sides. Place your feet shoulder-width apart. Jump to the side onto your right foot. At the same time, swing your left foot behind your right foot. Jump to the side onto your left foot and do the same. Continue for five to 10 minutes.

SHE'S GOT *Game*

In 2016 Californian Lois Austin played two to three volleyball games a day, three times each week. It's a lot of play—especially considering she was 80 years old.

How did she keep up with teammates and opponents 20 to 30 years younger? She credited her endurance to eating right, working out regularly, and thinking positively.

~ Tip ~

Add **cardiovascular** training to your workout routine to improve endurance. Try jogging or jumping rope.

cardiovascular—relating to the heart and blood vessels

Jump! Jump!

Volleyball players have many reasons to jump during a game. On offense, they jump up to attack the ball hard and win the point. Playing defense, they try to block the ball when their opponents hit it over the net. Increasing vertical jump height is a great way to get an edge on your opponent.

Vertical Jump Drills

Start improving your vertical jump by measuring your ability. Hold a piece of chalk in your hand. Stand next to an outside wall. Jump up and mark the wall with the chalk as high as you can. Use a tape measure to determine the height of your jump. Try jumping six times in a row every day without measuring. After a week, jump with chalk again to see if you've improved. Keep practicing, measuring your progress once a week.

Train for more height by jumping onto a sturdy bench or bleacher. Have a partner **spot** you to make sure you don't fall. Jump up and land on the platform with both feet. Jump continuously for 30 seconds daily. Try a higher platform when your coach says you are ready.

---

spot—assist

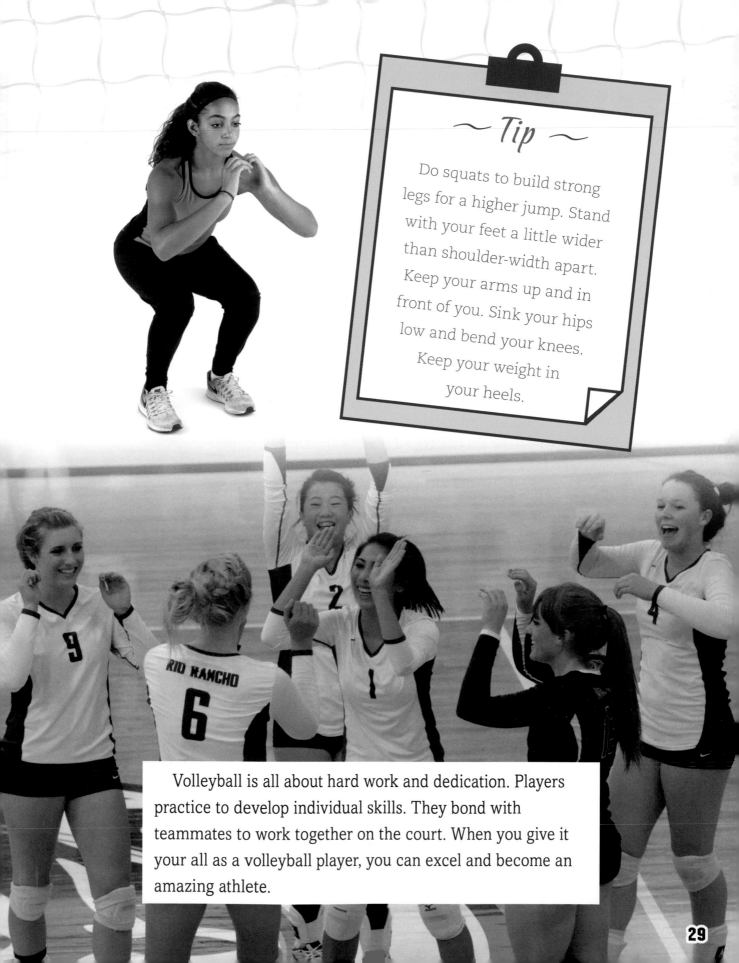

~Tip~

Do squats to build strong legs for a higher jump. Stand with your feet a little wider than shoulder-width apart. Keep your arms up and in front of you. Sink your hips low and bend your knees. Keep your weight in your heels.

Volleyball is all about hard work and dedication. Players practice to develop individual skills. They bond with teammates to work together on the court. When you give it your all as a volleyball player, you can excel and become an amazing athlete.

GLOSSARY

agile (AJ-ahyl)—able to move quickly and easily

attack (uh-TAK)—a forceful, overhand hit to return the ball over the net

cardiovascular (kahr-dee-oh-VAS-kyoo-luhr)—relating to the heart and blood vessels

dynamic (dye-NAM-ik)—involves motion

momentum (moh-MEN-tuhm)—the strength or force something has while it is moving

rally (RAL-ee)—the time between a serve and the end of play

set (SET)—a game played to a predetermined number of points

spot (SPOT)—assist

static (STAH-tik)—does not involve motion

tryout (TRY-OUT)—an event that tests athletes on their new skill, attitude, and potential in their sport

vertical (VUR-tuh-kuhl)—straight up and down

READ MORE

Doeden, Matt. *Volleyball.* Summer Olympic Sports. Mankato, Minn.: Amicus Ink, 2016.

Forest, Anne. *Girls Play Volleyball.* Girls Join the Team. New York, New York: PowerKids Press, 2016.

Suen, Anastasia. *A Girl's Guide to Volleyball.* Get in the Game. Mankato, Minn.: Capstone Press, 2012.

INTERNET SITES

FactHound offers a safe, fun way to find Internet sites related to this book. All of the sites on FactHound have been researched by our staff.

Here's all you do:
Visit *www.facthound.com*

Type in this code: **9781515747208**

Super-cool stuff! Check out projects, games and lots more at
www.capstonekids.com

INDEX